FROM RAMEN TO RICHES

Unlock Prosperity and Break Free From Financial Fears

TABLE OF CONTENTS

Part 1: Rewiring Your Money Mindset

Part 2: Putting Psychology into Practice

Part 3: Achieving Financial Peace

INTRODUCTION

Welcome to "From **Ramen to Riches: Unlock Prosperity and Break Free From Financial Fears**." In this empowering guide, we invite you on a transformative journey of regeneration, where we will rekindle your financial hopes and dreams, and help you flourish in a world of abundance and fulfillment.

Life is full of ups and downs, and it's not uncommon to find yourself in a place of financial struggle. Whether you're drowning in debt, living paycheck to paycheck, or haunted by constant worries about money, it's time to rewrite your story and regenerate your financial well-being.

Drawing upon proven strategies, practical wisdom, and a dash of inspiration, "From Ramen to Riches" will guide you through the process of rebuilding your financial foundation. We understand the challenges and fears that often accompany financial uncertainties, and we are here to provide you with the tools, knowledge, and mindset shifts needed to break free and thrive.

This book is not just about accumulating wealth; it's about a holistic regeneration of your financial life. We will take you on a journey of self-discovery, helping you understand your beliefs, attitudes, and behaviors towards money. By shedding light on limiting beliefs and replacing them with empowering mindsets, you will open the doors to new possibilities and create a roadmap for financial success.

Through "**From Ramen to Riches**," we will dive into the practical aspects of budgeting, saving, and investing. We will provide you with strategies to manage debt, establish healthy financial habits, and create a sustainable path toward wealth accumulation. From building an emergency fund to making smart investment decisions, you will learn how to navigate the financial landscape with confidence and resilience.

But regeneration goes beyond mere financial strategies. It is a transformation of your relationship with money and an alignment of your financial goals with your values and passions. We will guide you in identifying your true desires and weaving them into a prosperous and purposeful financial plan. You will gain the tools to make intentional spending decisions, cultivate a mindset of abundance, and design a life that reflects your deepest aspirations.

Are you ready to break free from the grip of financial fears and regenerate your financial reality?

Are you ready to unleash your true financial potential and create a life of abundance and fulfillment? If so, "**From Ramen to Riches**" is your roadmap. Together, let's embark on this journey of regeneration, reclaim your financial power, and unlock the prosperous future you deserve.

So, grab a pen, open your mind to **Unlock Prosperity and Break Free From Financial Fears**

Part 1: Rewiring Your Money Mindset

Chapter 1: The Money Myths Holding You Back

The clinking of coins in your pocket. The sound of crisp banknotes rustling in your wallet. Our society depends on money to fuel its aspirations and fulfill its needs. However, a thick mist of ignorance surrounds this essential energy for many. We hold onto antiquated ideas and misconceptions that harm our financial prospects and skew how we see abundance. Today, we dismantle each of these delusions one at a time to expose the raw reality underneath.

Myth 1: Money is scarce, a zero-sum game where one wins and another loses.

Imagine not a stagnant puddle, but a boundless ocean of wealth. Opportunities wait to be seized as they dance on its waves. This myth of scarcity betrays subtle falsehoods, such as the idea that wealth is a finite pie with insufficient portions for everyone and that your success depends on the failure of others. But take a deeper look. When invention is combined with creativity and teamwork, prosperity rises. Others can be empowered by your financial success, and vice versa. Escape the mentality of scarcity and welcome the boundless possibilities of an abundant, cooperative society.

Myth 2: Happiness is the ultimate goal, and money is merely a tool to achieve it.

We follow fads, lusting after the newest technology or the hottest status symbol, thinking they will bring us eternal happiness. However, the evidence presents a different image. Although having money is a must for happiness, the pursuit of material goods frequently leaves us empty and chases after unfulfilled dreams. Strong connections, worthwhile endeavors, and a feeling of purpose that goes beyond material possessions are the underlying sources of true happiness, we discover. While money can be an effective tool, use it as a servant rather than a master in your quest for true happiness.

Myth 3: The rich are simply luckier, blessed with advantages beyond your reach.

The allure of the rags-to-riches can be so compelling that it can make us forget about the innumerable people who have achieved money through hard work and perseverance. Granted, some people are born with an advantage, but luck tends to reward perseverance over privilege. Avoid comparing your starting position to the finish line of another person. The true competition is with your constraints, your dedication to development, and your capacity to pick up lessons from each setback. Climb your achievement ladder, step by step, and leave jealousy in your wake.

These are just the first cracks in the facade of money myths. In upcoming chapters, we'll dismantle more debilitating beliefs, revealing the path to a healthy money mindset, one where abundance feels achievable, happiness is a genuine pursuit, and your financial journey is paved with your unique determination.

Are you ready to shed the shackles of misconception and forge a new path to financial freedom? Then turn the page, because the treasure map lies within.

Chapter 2: From Scarcity to Abundance: Shifting Your Money Focus

Imagine your wallet shrinking every time you spend a dime. Scary, right? That's how our brains often act with money. We see it as a shrinking pie, a fight for crumbs. But what if we told you there's another way? A way where your wallet feels like a bottomless ocean, with riches just waiting to be discovered? That's the power of shifting your money focus from scarcity to abundance.

Ditch the Scarcity Mindset

Ever hoard groceries because you think the store ran out? That's scarcity thinking! You see money as a limited resource, a treasure chest you guard with fear. But here's the truth: opportunities to earn and grow your wealth are everywhere. Think of it like planting seeds – every effort, every skill, can blossom into financial abundance.

Embrace the Abundance Mindset

Picture a vast ocean, waves of possibilities sparking on its surface. That's the abundance mindset! You trust that there's enough for everyone, and your success doesn't come at someone else's cost. You focus on growth, on nurturing your skills and talents, knowing that your financial wellspring will keep filling.

Shifting Gears:

So, how do we make this mental magic happen? *Here are some tricks:*

Gratitude Magnet: Instead of counting what you lack, appreciate what you already have. A roof over your head? Food on the table? These are seeds of abundance! Expressing gratitude attracts more, like a money magnet.

Opportunity Seeker: Ditch the "nothing good ever happens to me" attitude! Train your eyes to see possibilities. Every new skill, every connection, is a wave carrying you toward financial shores.

Growth Mindset: Don't get stuck thinking "I'm not good enough." Believe you can learn, grow, and achieve. Invest in yourself, in your skills, and watch your abundance bloom.

Shifting your money focus is a journey, not a destination. There will be bumps, but every step, every new belief, takes you closer to that ocean of wealth.

Chapter 3: Taming the Inner Gambler: Why We Make Bad Financial Decisions

We all want to be smart with our money, right? Invest wisely, save consistently, and build a secure future. But sometimes, this tiny voice inside shouts, "YOLO!" or "Double down!", leading us to financial decisions that make future users groan. Let's face it, we all have this inner gambler, and understanding why he whispers tempting nonsense is key to taming him and making smarter financial choices.

Meet the Inner Gambler

He's that impulsive cousin of logic, fueled by instant gratification and "what if?" scenarios. He loves the thrill of a quick win, whether it's buying lottery tickets or taking a chance on a risky investment. But here's the catch: his wins are fleeting, often overshadowed by losses that leave us scrambling.

Why He Wins Sometimes

Our brains are wired for rewards, and the rush of a potential win activates our pleasure centers. This dopamine hit, even for insignificant gains, reinforces the gambling behavior. Think of it like a slot machine – occasional small wins keep us pulling the lever, hoping for the jackpot that rarely comes.

Taming the Beast

Don't get us wrong, the inner gambler isn't all bad. He can push us outside our comfort zones, try new things, and take calculated risks. But the key is to keep him on a leash, under the control of our rational brain. *Here are some tips:*

Delay the Decision: When the gambler whispers "Buy now!", take a timeout. Sleep on it, research it, and let logic weigh in. Often, the morning light shines a different light on impulsive choices.

Plan, Budget, Stick to the Script: Having a clear financial plan takes the guesswork out of spending. Your budget is your roadmap, and the gambler doesn't get to choose the detours!

Focus on Long-Term Gains: Remind yourself that true financial success is a marathon, not a sprint. Small, consistent choices that build wealth over time beat risky bets any day.

Reward Yourself Strategically: Don't deny yourself all the fun! Instead of gambling wins, reward yourself for sticking to your financial plan. A concert ticket for reaching a savings goal feels much better than a lottery ticket spent in vain.

Taming the inner gambler is a continuous process. There will be stumbles and moments of temptation, but with awareness and these tools, you can keep him in check and make financial decisions that your future self will thank you for.

So, embrace the calculated risk-taker within, but keep the impulsive gambler on a tight leash, and watch your financial journey turn from a rollercoaster ride to a smooth, steady climb towards success.

Chapter 4: The Psychology of Saving: Stop Procrastinating, Build Wealth

Saving money - it's like exercise for your finances. You know it's good for you, but getting started can feel like climbing Mount Everest in flip-flops. We put it off, prioritize instant gratification, and before we know it, retirement feels like a distant mirage. But what if we told you saving could be less like a chore and more like a treasure hunt, uncovering a stash of future freedom with each deposit? Let's delve into the psychology of saving and learn how to ditch the procrastination monster, building wealth one step at a time.

Why We Procrastinate

Future is fuzzy: Retirement, buying a house, those feel like far-off dreams. Our brains love instant gratification, and saving rewards seem hazy compared to the "buy now" button's dopamine rush.

Loss aversion: Seeing an empty bank account feels scary, even if it's temporary.

We'd rather spend what we have than "lose" some to savings, even though that "loss" will grow into future gains.

Lack of clarity: What even counts as "saving"? How much is enough? Without clear goals and plans, the saving journey feels overwhelming and directionless.

Shifting Your Mindset

Reframe the narrative: Think of saving as investing in your future self, the one who deserves that dream house or a worry-free retirement. It's not about deprivation, it's about building a brighter tomorrow.

Make it tangible: Set short-term goals, like saving for a vacation or a new gadget. Celebrating these milestones fuels your motivation and shows you the power of consistent saving.

Automate the process: Set up automatic transfers to your savings account. Once it's out of sight, out of mind (and temptation!), your future self will thank you for this effortless wealth-building.

Saving Hacks for Procrastinators

Round it up: Round up every purchase to the nearest dollar or ten and watch those savings add up effortlessly. Every coffee becomes a future investment!

Challenge yourself: Dare yourself to save a certain amount each day or week. Turn it into a game, track your progress, and reward yourself for sticking to it.

Find savings partners: Team up with friends or family and support each other's saving goals. Share tips, track your progress together, and celebrate each other's wins.

Saving doesn't have to be a painful marathon. By understanding the psychology behind procrastination and implementing these smart hacks, you can turn it into a rewarding journey, one brick at a time building your financial fortress.

Start small, celebrate milestones, and watch your future self bask in the sunshine of your wise choices.

Chapter 5: Ditching the Joneses: Why Keeping Up is a Race You Can't Win

Scrolling through social media, bombarded with images of vacations on yachts, designer wardrobes, and sparkling new cars. The voice whispers, "They have it all, why not you?" This, my friends, is the "Keeping Up with the Joneses" trap, a dangerous game that can wreak havoc on your finances and your mental well-being. Today, we expose its tricks and equip you with tools to break free, paving your path to financial happiness.

The Joneses: Masters of Illusion

Let's be real, the Joneses' lives are often carefully curated facades. They might be drowning in debt, living paycheck to paycheck, but they'll never post that picture. Social media is a highlight reel, not a reality show. Comparing your behind-the-scenes struggles to their carefully crafted spotlights is a recipe for envy and financial distress.

The Perils of Comparison

Chasing a Moving Target: The Joneses are constantly upgrading, their "having it all" bar forever rising. Trying to keep up is like chasing a treadmill at high speed – you'll never reach the finish line.

Financial Strain: The pressure to match the Joneses can lead to impulsive spending, draining your bank account and sacrificing long-term financial goals.

Dwindling Self-Esteem: Constantly comparing yourself to others is a surefire way to erode your self-worth. Focus on your progress, not someone else's curated image.

Breaking Free from the Trap

Gratitude Magnet: Instead of coveting what others have, appreciate what you do. Practice gratitude for your blessings, big and small. A grateful heart finds joy in abundance, not comparison.

Values Compass: Define your values and goals. What matters to you? Financial security? Travel? Helping others? Focusing on your unique path drowns out the noise of the Joneses' siren song.

Celebrate Your Wins: Track your progress, no matter how small. Saving for a down payment? Paid off a credit card? Every step towards your goals is a victory worth celebrating.

The Joneses are a distraction, not a destination. Their lives have little bearing on your journey. Focus on building a life that aligns with your values, a life you can be proud of, not one dictated by envy and comparison.

Embrace your unique path, celebrate your wins, and watch your financial story unfold beautifully, one chapter at a time.

Part 2: Putting Psychology into Practice

Chapter 6: Spending vs. Investing: Mapping Your Money Mindset

Our wallets hold more than just coins and bills; they carry stories. Stories of priorities, values, and dreams. But sometimes, those stories get tangled, blurring the lines between spending and investing. This chapter is your financial GPS, guiding you through the landscape of choices, helping you decipher your money mindset, and charting a course toward a fulfilling financial future.

The Spending Spree vs. The Investment Oasis

The Spending Spree: Instant gratification beckons, whispering sweet nothings about the latest gadgets, trendy clothes, and fleeting experiences. It's a dopamine rush in the wallet but often leaves behind a trail of temporary satisfaction and dwindling resources.

The Investment Oasis: This path focuses on delayed gratification, nurturing long-term growth, and building towards future goals. It requires patience and foresight but rewards you with financial security, freedom, and the ability to chase bigger dreams.

Understanding Your Money Story

Track Your Spending: Where does your money flow? Analyze your past few months' expenses. Does your spending align with your values and goals? Are there habits or categories draining your resources? Awareness is the first step to change.

Define Your Values: What truly matters to you? Experiences, security, helping others? Identifying your core values helps you prioritize spending that aligns with your life's vision.

Dream Big, Plan Smart: Picture your ideal future - financial freedom, travel, early retirement? Translate those dreams into concrete goals, then break them down into actionable steps. Your spending plan becomes your roadmap to those dreams.

Investing in Yourself

The most valuable investment you can make is in yourself. *Consider these "future-proof" purchases:*

Skills and knowledge: Education, courses, workshops - anything that expands your abilities and earning potential.

Health and well-being: Gym memberships, healthy food choices, preventive healthcare - investments in your physical and mental well-being pay dividends for life.

Relationships: Strengthening bonds with loved ones, and building a supportive network - true wealth lies in strong connections that enrich your life in countless ways.

This isn't about depriving yourself or living like a hermit. It's about conscious spending, and making choices that align with your long-term goals and values.

Treat your money like a precious resource, an investment in your future self. Celebrate responsible spending, savor the joy of delayed gratification, and watch your financial story unfold as a compelling narrative of growth, freedom, and fulfillment.

Chapter 7: The Value of Delay: Patience, Your Financial Superpower

In our fast-paced world, instant gratification reigns supreme. We want it all, and we want it now. This "get-rich-quick" mentality spills over into our finances, tempting us with impulsive purchases, risky investments, and the seductive whispers of credit card debt. But what if we told you the key to financial success lies not in speed, but in a quiet superpower called patience?

Think of patience as your financial kryptonite, banishing the demons of impulsive spending and short-sighted decisions. It's the superpower that lets you see beyond the immediate and choose long-term value over fleeting thrills.

The Allure of Instant Gratification

Dopamine Rush: That surge of pleasure from a new purchase. The thrill of a risky investment. These temporary highs cloud our judgment, leading to choices that might benefit our "now" selves but cripple our futures.

Keeping Up with the Joneses: Social media bombards us with images of instant affluence, fueling desires to emulate lifestyles we may not be able to afford. Comparing our progress to someone else's highlight reel is a recipe for financial anxiety and impulsive spending.

Fear of Missing Out (FOMO): We see deals expiring, discounts vanishing, and fear we'll miss out on the "perfect" opportunity. This FOMO often pushes us into hasty decisions with long-term consequences.

Why Patience Wins

Compounding Power: Patience lets you leverage the magic of compound interest. Saving now, even small amounts, can grow significantly over time, building a secure financial future for your older self.

Informed Decisions: Delaying gives you time to research, compare, and analyze. It allows you to avoid impulsive purchases and make smarter investments based on logic, not fleeting desires.

Freedom from Debt: Impatience often leads to credit card debt, a financial quicksand that can trap you in a cycle of high interest and missed payments. Patience empowers you to plan purchases, save responsibly, and break free from the shackles of debt.

Cultivating Your Patience Muscle

Gratitude Practice: Appreciate what you already have, no matter how small. This shifts your focus from "lack" to "abundance," making you less susceptible to the lure of instant gratification.

Goal Setting: Define your long-term financial goals, whether it's a down payment on a house, a dream vacation, or early retirement. Having a clear vision keeps you motivated and helps you resist short-term temptations.

Delayed Rewards: Celebrate milestones and achievements, but choose rewards that don't involve immediate spending. A walk in nature, a picnic with friends, or simply savoring the satisfaction of reaching a goal can be equally fulfilling without draining your wallet.

Patience is not about deprivation or living a life of asceticism. It's about conscious control over your spending, and making deliberate choices that align with your long-term goals and values.

Embrace the power of delay, nurture your patience muscle, and watch your financial journey transform from a frantic sprint to a steady, purposeful climb toward lasting success.

Chapter 8: Build Your Blueprint, Not a Budget: Automating Your Path to Financial Freedom

Budgets can feel like shackles, rigid constraints that stifle spontaneity and freedom. But what if we told you there's a better way? A way to achieve financial well-being without feeling like you're constantly counting pennies? Enter the world of systems, your personalized financial autopilot that sets you on a course toward success without a single spreadsheet in sight.

Ditch the Budget, Embrace the System

Budgets often feel restrictive, temporary fixes to our spending habits. Systems, on the other hand, are like sturdy bridges, designed to carry you across the river of financial uncertainty to reach your long-term goals. They're about automation, proactive planning, and setting up habits that work for you, not against you.

Building Your Financial Blueprint

Know Yourself: Analyze your spending habits, identify your triggers, and understand your comfort zones. This self-awareness forms the foundation of your system.

Define Your Goals: Where do you want to be financially in 5, 10, or 20 years? Articulate clear, specific goals that motivate you and act as guiding stars for your system.

Automate Like a Pro: Set up automatic transfers to savings accounts, automate bill payments, and leverage technology to streamline your financial management. Let technology work for you, not the other way around.

Pay Yourself First: Treat saving like a mandatory bill. Allocate a fixed percentage of your income to savings immediately, before you even see the remaining balance. This ensures your future gets funded first, without relying on willpower.

Track Without Tears: Monitor your progress regularly, but without the stress of daily tracking. Choose simple methods like monthly check-ins or automated reports that give you a clear picture of your financial health without sacrificing your sanity.

Systems are built to evolve, not fossilize. As your income, goals, and life circumstances change, adapt your system accordingly. Flexibility is key to its long-term effectiveness.

Benefits of the System Approach

Reduced Stress: Automation minimizes time spent managing finances, freeing you from budgeting anxieties and focusing on what truly matters.

Consistency is Key: Systems built into your routine become almost subconscious, ensuring you stay on track toward your goals without constant willpower or effort.

Freedom with a Net: Enjoy spontaneous fun and occasional splurges, knowing your system acts as a safety net, guiding your finances back on track.

So, put down the budget spreadsheet and pick up the blueprint for your financial future.

Design a system that works for you, automate your path to success, and watch your bank account transform from a source of stress to a springboard for freedom and fulfillment.

Chapter 9: Risk and Reward: Dancing with Uncertainty (and Winning the Waltz)

Life's a waltz, a mesmerizing dance between the familiar and the unknown. Every step forward, every decision we make, holds the potential for both breathtaking rewards and unexpected stumbles. It's at this stage, in the intricate interplay of risk and reward, that our financial destiny unfolds.

We've all heard the warnings: "Avoid risk, play it safe," they echo. But true growth, true financial freedom, often lies beyond the comfort zone, bathed in the moonlight of uncertainty. This chapter isn't about reckless leaps or blind gambling; it's about embracing the inherent dance of risk and reward, learning to navigate its rhythm with calculated steps and open hearts.

Understanding the Two Faces of Risk

The Shadow: There's the fear, the paralysis, the voice whispering "what if" until it drowns out any chance of progress.

This is the negative face of risk, the one that keeps us chained to the shore, afraid to dip our toes in the ocean of possibilities.

The Light: But risk also holds the key to exhilarating growth, to reach beyond our perceived limitations. It's the catalyst for innovation, the fuel for achieving dreams that seemed impossible when viewed from the safety of the familiar.

Mastering the Waltz

Know Your Threshold: We all have different risk tolerances. Some find comfort in stability, others crave the thrill of the unknown. Define your comfort zone, understand your risk appetite, and dance within that space.

Measure Every Move: Before leaping, analyze the potential rewards and pitfalls. Research, gather information, and weigh the potential outcomes. Make informed decisions, not impulsive jumps.

Diversify Your Steps: Don't put all your eggs in one basket. Spread your investments, explore different opportunities, and avoid relying on a single, high-risk venture.

Prepare for the Dip: No waltz is without an unexpected turn. Build a financial safety net, an emergency fund that can cushion the blow of an unexpected stumble.

Embrace the Learning Curve: Risks, even calculated ones, can sometimes lead to setbacks. But view these as lessons, stepping stones on your path to financial mastery. Learn from them, adjust your approach, and keep dancing.

Embracing risk isn't about recklessness; it's about calculated courage, about stepping outside your comfort zone with intention and awareness. It's about learning to trust your rhythm, to find the perfect balance between caution and curiosity, and ultimately turn the potential pitfalls of risk into the exhilarating grace of financial reward.

Chapter 10: Money and the Tango: Navigating Finances with Family and Friends

The lifeblood of society, the fuel of dreams, and the occasional landmine in the delicate landscape of relationships. When it comes to family and friends, finances can become a tricky tango, a dance of expectations, obligations, and sometimes, awkward silences. But fear not, dear reader, for this chapter, is your guide to navigating this financial tango with grace and understanding.

The Tangled Web of Money and Relationships

Loans and Expectations: Borrowing from loved ones can be a blessing or a burden, depending on clear communication and realistic expectations. Set terms, discuss timelines, and avoid letting unspoken assumptions cloud the dance.

Financial Disparities: Different income levels within a family or friend group can create tension. Embrace open communication, avoid comparisons, and celebrate each other's successes, regardless of the numbers in their bank accounts.

Gifts and the Burden of Obligation: Gift-giving can be a joyous expression of love, but it can also create pressure and resentment. Define your comfort level, set boundaries, and remember that true affection doesn't require a price tag.

Steps for a Smooth Financial Tango

Open Communication is Key: Talk about money openly and honestly. Discuss budgets, expectations, and potential concerns before they become stumbling blocks. Clear communication is the essential lubricant for any financial tango.

Respectful Boundaries: Understand your own and your loved ones' financial boundaries. Don't overstep or make assumptions, and be prepared to politely decline requests that don't align with your comfort level.

Focus on Shared Values: Money shouldn't define your relationships. Prioritize shared experiences, quality time, and mutual support over financial considerations. Remember, memories and laughter are the true treasures, not the digits in a bank account.

Seek Professional Advice if Needed: Complex financial situations may require professional guidance. Don't hesitate to involve a financial advisor or counselor to help navigate difficult conversations or create fair financial agreements.

Celebrate Each Other's Successes: Support your loved ones in their financial journeys, regardless of their goals or circumstances. Celebrate their achievements, offer encouragement during challenges, and remember, their success doesn't diminish yours.

The financial tango with family and friends is a continuous dance, requiring flexibility, understanding, and a healthy dose of communication.

By following these steps, you can turn potential pitfalls into opportunities for connection, strengthen your bonds, and ensure that money never overshadows the true value of your relationships.

The most beautiful financial tangos are built on trust, respect, and the understanding that true wealth lies not in numbers, but in the shared moments and unwavering support we offer each other.

Part 3: Achieving Financial Peace

Chapter 11: From Hustle to Flow: Embracing Joy in Your Financial Journey

We've traversed the terrain of mindset shifts, strategized savings plans, and waltzed with the uncertainties of risk. Now, in this chapter, we arrive at a destination often sought, yet seldom truly reached: financial peace. But here's the secret: financial peace isn't a static state, it's a dance of flow in your financial journey. It's not about reaching a fixed number in your bank account, but about finding joy and purpose within the very act of managing your finances.

Ditch the Hustle, Embrace the Flow

The Hustle Trap: We chase numbers, climb career ladders, and hustle constantly, believing financial security lies at the summit. But this can lead to burnout, anxiety, and a disconnect from the present moment.

The Flow Dance: Financial Peace invites you to step onto a different stage. It's where your financial choices align with your values and aspirations, where you find meaning and purpose in managing your money.

Steps to the Flow Dance

Reconnecting with Values: What truly matters to you? Family, travel, helping others? Define your core values and let them guide your financial decisions. When your money aligns with your values, it ceases to be a burden and becomes a tool for achieving your dreams.

Gratitude as Currency: Shift your focus from "lack" to "abundance." Appreciate what you have, no matter how small. Practice gratitude, and watch your financial journey become a source of joy, not constant striving.

Small Wins, Big Rewards: Celebrate milestones, no matter how seemingly insignificant. Saving for a weekend getaway, paying off a small debt, or simply sticking to your budget are all victories worth acknowledging. Celebrate the process, not just the destination.

Finding Purpose in Giving: Money isn't just about acquiring; it's also about sharing. Invest in causes you care about, support loved ones, or volunteer your time. When you use your resources to make a positive impact, your financial journey takes on a whole new level of meaning.

Learning and Growing: Embrace financial education as a lifelong pursuit. Read books, attend workshops, and seek guidance from experts. The more you learn, the more confident and empowered you become in managing your finances.

Financial peace isn't a destination, it's a continuous journey. There will be bumps, detours, and unexpected turns. But by embracing the flow, prioritizing joy and purpose, and aligning your finances with your values, you can transform your financial journey from a relentless hustle into a graceful dance, filled with meaning and the ever-present satisfaction of progress.

It's not about the amount in your bank account, but the joy you find in the dance itself. And in that flow, you'll discover that true financial peace lies not in a fixed number, but in the harmonious blend of purpose, meaning, and a sprinkle of financial wisdom.

Chapter 12: The Financial Force Field: Staying Grounded When Markets Go Wild

Imagine standing on a cliff during a hurricane. The wind howls, waves crash, and the ground beneath your feet seems to tremble. This, my friends, is the metaphor for navigating the unpredictable terrain of financial markets. Volatility, it seems, is the constant weather pattern, with gusts of panic and dips of despair threatening to sweep you off course. But fear not, intrepid investor! This chapter equips you with the mental force field – a shield of knowledge and perspective – to stand strong amidst the financial mayhem.

The Siren Song of Panic

FOMO and the Fear of Missing Out: Market surges trigger envy, urging you to jump in and chase potential gains, often leading to impulsive, uninformed decisions.

Loss Aversion Bites: Seeing red numbers activates our primal fear of loss, prompting knee-jerk reactions like selling at a loss to avoid further pain.

The Echo Chamber of Anxiety: News outlets amplify volatility, painting a picture of impending doom, fueling panic and irrational decision-making.

Building Your Mental Force Field

Invest in Knowledge: Equip yourself with financial literacy. Understand market cycles, asset classes, and diversification strategies. Knowledge is your anchor in the storm, calming your nerves and guiding informed decisions.

Set Realistic Goals: Chasing quick wins is a recipe for disaster. Define long-term goals aligned with your risk tolerance and investment horizon. This long-term view helps you weather temporary fluctuations without derailing your course.

Tune Out the Noise: Don't let market headlines dictate your actions. Limit your exposure to financial news and focus on your plan. Remember, temporary dips don't negate your long-term strategy.

Diversify Like a Pro: Don't put all your eggs in one basket. Spread your investments across different asset classes and sectors. This diversification acts as a shock absorber, mitigating the impact of market swings.

Revisit, Rebalance, Repeat: Regularly review your portfolio and adjust your investments as needed to align with your evolving goals and risk appetite. This proactive approach keeps your strategy relevant and resilient.

Volatility is inevitable, but panic is optional. By equipping yourself with knowledge, setting clear goals, and adopting a long-term perspective, you can navigate market upheavals with composure and confidence.

Treat volatility as a dance, not a disaster. Stay grounded in your strategy, avoid emotional decisions, and trust the power of time and diversification to see you through even the wildest storms.

Raise your force field of financial wisdom, stand tall amidst the market winds, and remember, true wealth lies not in avoiding volatility, but in navigating it with grace, knowledge, and a healthy dose of perspective.

As you emerge from the storm, stronger and wiser, you'll realize that the calm seas of financial peace aren't the absence of waves, but the ability to ride them with confidence and a steady hand on the tiller.

Chapter 13: Building a Legacy: The Tapestry Woven Beyond Numbers

We've journeyed through the labyrinth of finances, conquered the dragons of debt, and danced with the unpredictable winds of the market. Now, in this chapter, we reach a destination beyond mere accumulation – a place where wealth transcends numbers and takes shape as a legacy.

This isn't about the cold clink of coins or the envy-inducing gleam of a mansion; it's about the richness woven into the tapestry of your life, the impact you leave on the world, and the stories whispered long after you've danced under the setting sun.

From Numbers to Tapestry

The Glittering Illusion: Financial success, if measured solely by material possessions, is fleeting and fragile. A twist of fate, a market crash, and the carefully constructed facade can crumble, leaving behind a hollow victory.

Weaving the True Canvas: True wealth lies in the threads we weave into the fabric of our lives. It's the love we cultivate, the knowledge we share, the positive footprints we leave on the sands of time.

Unraveling the Threads of Legacy

The Thread of Relationships: Nurture your connections, build bridges of love and support, and watch your legacy bloom in the hearts of those you cherish. The memories you create, the laughter you share, become an inheritance far more valuable than any bank account.

The Thread of Knowledge: Share your wisdom, mentor others, and leave the world a little brighter with the knowledge you've gleaned. Every life touched, every mind ignited, adds a vibrant thread to the tapestry of your legacy.

The Thread of Contribution: Lend a hand, champion a cause, and let your actions ripple outwards, painting the world with a splash of hope and positive change. Each act of kindness, each barrier broken, weaves a legacy stronger than any monument.

The Thread of Living Your Truth: Embrace your passions, pursue your dreams, and dance to the beat of your drum. The authenticity you radiate, the joy you inspire, becomes a beacon of inspiration, a legacy that lives on in the hearts of those who witnessed your vibrant dance.

Legacy isn't built in marble or engraved on gold; it's woven into the very fabric of our lives, in the whispers of laughter, the echoes of shared experiences, and the ripples of positive change we set in motion. It's about embracing the tapestry of life, beyond the limitations of numbers, and leaving behind a story worth telling, a legacy worth singing about.

Embrace the threads of love, knowledge, and contribution, and let your life be a symphony of positive impact. For in the end, the truest measure of wealth is not what you acquire, but what you leave behind – a legacy woven with purpose, passion, and the everlasting threads of a life well-lived.

Chapter 14: Enough is Enough: Finding and Celebrating Financial Freedom

Build budgets and spreadsheets in their name. But what if we told you "enough" isn't a number at all? What if it's a feeling, a state of being born not from accumulation, but from a profound shift in perspective? This is the chapter where we rewrite the definition of "enough" and celebrate the true dance of financial freedom.

Redefining Enough

The Shifting Sands of Numbers: Chasing a specific financial target is a never-ending game, with the goalposts constantly shifting under our feet. True freedom lies not in reaching a number, but in finding contentment with enough for your needs, values, and dreams.

Gratitude, the Secret Weapon: Cultivate gratitude for what you already have, no matter how small. Shift your focus from "lack" to "abundance," and watch your perception of "enough" expand like a blossoming flower.

Beyond the Material: Remember, true wealth isn't confined to bank accounts. It's measured in the richness of your experiences, the strength of your relationships, and the joy you find in everyday moments.

Finding the Freedom Dance

Align Your Spending with Values: Make your money dance to the tune of your values. Prioritize experiences that resonate with you, support causes you to believe in, and invest in relationships that enrich your life. When your spending aligns with your values, "enough" feels closer than you think.

Simplify and Savor: Let go of the need for excess. Embrace minimalism, declutter your life, and learn to savor the simple pleasures. The freedom found in living with less is a treasure often overlooked.

Time, the True Luxury: Don't let chasing money steal your most precious resource –

time. Prioritize experiences over possessions, cultivate hobbies that bring joy, and learn to savor the present moment. In the abundance of time, you'll discover a freedom more valuable than any bank account.

Celebrate Milestones, Not Just Goals: Don't wait for the mythical "enough" to celebrate. Acknowledge and appreciate the progress you've made, and the small victories along the way. Every step towards your financial goals is a reason to dance with joy.

Financial freedom isn't about accumulating mountains of gold; it's about finding contentment, living with purpose, and building a life that truly resonates with you. It's a daily dance, a conscious choice to focus on what truly matters, and a deep understanding that enough, in its most profound form, lies not in numbers, but in the richness of your experiences and the freedom of your soul.

So, take a deep breath, release the grip of chasing external numbers, and step onto the dance floor of self-discovery.

Embrace gratitude, align your spending with your values, savor the simple joys, and celebrate every step of your journey. In the end, the truest financial freedom is found not in reaching a destination, but in enjoying the dance itself. And when you learn to do that, you'll discover that enough was always within you, waiting to be embraced.

Chapter 15: Money Can't Buy Everything, But It Can Buy (Some) Happiness

"Money can't buy happiness." It's a mantra whispered at family gatherings, a cautionary tale in movies, and a well-worn defense when someone flaunts their latest acquisition. But is it entirely true? Can money, the cold, hard stuff, really have no role in crafting a joyful life?

It's not about glorifying materialism or painting riches as the sole ticket to bliss. Instead, it's about acknowledging the nuanced, complex relationship between money and happiness, a tango where both partners play a role, albeit with different steps and varying degrees of influence.

Money and Happiness: A Nuanced Tango

Beyond the Basics: Yes, the most pressing needs of sustenance, shelter, and healthcare must be met before happiness can even bloom. Maslow's pyramid reminds us that these foundational elements are the soil from which happiness can sprout.

Beyond the Bling: But that's not the end of the story. While a shiny new car or a luxurious vacation might bring a rush of excitement, research suggests it's fleeting. True happiness, the kind that endures, stems from deeper sources – meaningful relationships, personal growth, and a sense of purpose.

Money as a Tool: However, we can't discount the fact that money can be a powerful tool in pursuit of these deeper joys. It can buy experiences that strengthen bonds with loved ones, fuel personal growth through education or travel, and support causes that give life meaning.

Dancing with Financial Joy

Financial Security as a Stepping Stone: Imagine happiness as a vibrant garden. Financial security acts as a sturdy fence, keeping worries at bay and allowing the flowers of joy to flourish without the constant threat of weeds like debt or unexpected expenses.

Investing in Experiences: Material possessions often depreciate, but experiences tend to appreciate value, enriching our lives with memories and stories. Use your resources to create shared adventures, pursue passions, and connect with the world around you.

Giving as a Source of Joy: Sharing your wealth, supporting others, and contributing to causes you care about can unlock a profound sense of happiness that transcends the limitations of personal gain. Giving fosters connection expands your perspective, and adds a powerful beat to the happiness tango.

Money, on its own, is not the elixir of happiness. It can be a useful tool, a facilitator, but it's not the magician pulling the rabbits out of hats.

True happiness arises from a complex interplay of factors, with money perhaps playing the role of a skilled orchestra conductor, orchestrating resources to amplify the inherent potential for joy within each of us.

Let's move beyond the simplistic pronouncements and embrace the nuanced waltz between money and happiness.

Use your resources wisely, invest in experiences and relationships, and don't neglect the powerful joy of giving.

It's not about the amount in your bank account, but the music you create with your financial choices. In that harmonious blend, you might just discover a happiness that transcends the limitations of numbers and fills your life with a symphony of fulfillment.

CONCLUSION

As we conclude the journey through "**From Ramen to Riches: Unlock Prosperity and Break Free From Financial Fears**," we hope you feel empowered and inspired to embark on a new chapter of financial growth and abundance. This book has equipped you with the knowledge, strategies, and mindset shifts necessary to regenerate your financial well-being and reclaim your financial power.

Throughout these pages, we have explored the practical aspects of budgeting, saving, investing, and managing debt. We have emphasized the importance of financial literacy and making informed decisions to create a solid foundation for your financial success.

By implementing these strategies, you will find yourself gradually breaking free from the cycle of financial constraints and living a life of financial freedom.

But "**From Ramen to Riches**" is not just about numbers and financial strategies; it is about a fundamental shift in your relationship with money.

We have delved into the mindset and psychology behind financial success, helping you identify and overcome limiting beliefs that have held you back in the past.

By embracing an abundant mindset and aligning your financial actions with your deepest values and aspirations, you have the power to create a life that is not only financially prosperous but also deeply fulfilling and purposeful.

It is important to remember that your financial journey is unique and ongoing. Be patient and kind to yourself as you navigate the ups and downs. Celebrate even the smallest of victories along the way, and maintain the determination and resilience to overcome any obstacles that may arise. Keep learning, seeking knowledge, and adapting to the ever-changing financial landscape.

As you move forward, continue to prioritize self-care, financial planning, and intentional decision-making. Regularly assess your progress, adjust your strategies if needed, and stay committed to your goals and dreams.

Remember, true wealth encompasses more than just money; it includes the freedom to live a life aligned with your passions, meaningful connections, and the ability to make a positive impact on the world around you.

Congratulations on completing this transformative journey! You have taken an important step towards breaking free from financial fears and embracing a life of prosperity. Now, armed with the knowledge and tools shared in this book, go forth and unleash your financial potential.

May your path to riches be filled with abundance, joy, and fulfillment. Embrace the opportunities that come your way, and never lose sight of the incredible potential that lies within you. Your journey from **"Ramen to Riches"** is a testament to your resilience, and we do not doubt that you will continue.

THANK YOU FOR READING!

www.ingramcontent.com/pod-product-compliance
Lightning Source LLC
Chambersburg PA
CBHW062250290526
45794CB00006B/2488